D0575793

COWGIRL ALPHABET

COWGIRL ALPHABET

Written by
Laurie Lazzaro Knowlton

Illustrated by Kathy Coates

PELICAN PUBLISHING COMPANY
GRETNA 2011

For my cowgirls, Charlotte and Kelsey—L. L. K.

Copyright © 2011
By Laurie Lazzaro Knowlton

Illustrations copyright © 2011
By Kathy Coates
All rights reserved

*The word "Pelican" and the depiction of a pelican
are trademarks of Pelican Publishing Company, Inc.,
and are registered in the U.S. Patent and Trademark Office.*

Library of Congress Cataloging-in-Publication Data

Knowlton, Laurie Lazzaro.
  Cowgirl alphabet / by Laurie Lazzaro Knowlton ; illustrated by Kathy
Coates.
      p. cm.
  ISBN 978-1-58980-669-6 (hardcover : alk. paper) 1. Cowgirls—West
(U.S.)—Juvenile literature. 2. West (U.S.)—Social life and customs—
Juvenile literature. 3. Alphabet books—Juvenile literature. I. Coates,
Kathy, ill. II. Title.
  F596.K63 2009
  978'.034—dc22
                        2009003958

Printed in Singapore
Published by Pelican Publishing Company, Inc.
1000 Burmaster Street, Gretna, Louisiana 70053

COWGIRL ALPHABET

A is for all-American girls.

Cowgirls are all-American girls between **A**bilene and **A**nnapolis, **A**labama and **A**laska, with a passion for horses and a love of country.

B is for beautiful boots.

Cowgirls wear **b**ig hats, **b**eaded vests, **b**right bandannas, **b**uckskin riding gloves, **b**rassy belts, **b**lue-jean **b**ritches, **b**atwing chaps, and **b**eautiful **b**oots.

C is for cowgirls.

Cowgirls come about by being confident gals who make a conscious decision to live life working cattle, raising colts, and loving their cowponies.

D is for dawn to dusk.

Cowgirls are determined to do everything better than cowboys do! Cowgirls can doctor a calf in Dallas at dawn and then perform death-defying stunts in Denver by dusk.

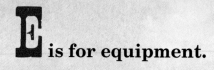

E is for equipment.

A cowgirl's equipment is called her tack. Every cowgirl owns a comfortable saddle. Educated cowgirls know to check their tack to make sure it is clean of burs and such.

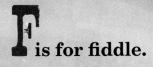

F is for fiddle.

A fiddle on its own will get a boot tapping, but a fiddle, guitar, and some cowgirls and cowboys, mixed up like a pot of stew, can lead to a real hoedown.

G is for the golden rule.

Good grooming, good manners, the golden rule, and grace before grub are a cowgirl's code of conduct.

H is for horse.

Hardworking cowgirls **h**old their **h**orses in **h**ighest regard. **H**ealthy **h**orses are **h**appy **h**orses. **H**ere's **h**ow to keep your **h**orse **h**appy!

✓ FEED
✓ WATER
✓ BRUSH
✓ PICK HOOVES
✓ MUCK STALL
✓ EXERCISE
✓ VACCINATIONS

I is for ironing.

A cowgirl **i**nsists that everything be in apple-pie order, whether she is **i**roning her dress shirt or **i**roning out the kinks of a rough-riding horse.

J is for johnnycakes.

Cowgirls are born eating johnnycakes made on a griddle over an open campfire. Sometimes a side of **jerky** is served, cut with a **jackknife**.

K is for kerchief.

A cowgirl's **k**erchief comes in mighty handy. "**K**erchief," "neckerchief," "handkerchief," or bandanna—that twenty-two-by-twenty-two-inch square of cotton material has darn near as many names as uses. A **k**erchief protects the mouth and nose from trail dust. It can also be used as a washcloth, coin pouch, or blindfold for a skittish horse.

L is for lasso.

Lasso, lariat, reata, and rope—they all add up to the same thing, a cowgirl's most important tool. A lasso's first job in the morning is to rope the cowgirl's mount of the day. Things get interesting when she lassos a cow from a bog and cuts a lone calf from a large herd. And when she's hankerin' for a little excitement, she'll lasso and break a wild horse.

M is for measuring by hands.

A cowgirl tells how tall her **m**are is by **m**easuring by hands. Way back when, cowgirls and cowboys realized that hand sizes were as different as a **m**ule from a **m**ouse. So they put their heads together and decided that one hand would be four inches. Horses range in size from four and a half hands to nineteen hands and three and a half inches.

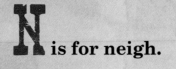 **is for neigh.**

A cowgirl's horse communicates with a **n**eigh, **n**icker, **n**uzzle, or **n**od. Being a good listener is a cowgirl's job. A high-pitched **n**eigh means, "I'm scared!" A softer **n**eigh means, "Howdy, pardner!" Then there is the **n**icker, a throaty sound that means, "Mighty glad to see you! Have any carrots?" If your horse **n**uzzles you, it means, "Did you bring me a surprise?" Listening and learning horse talk makes for good friends.

O is for old wish books.

"Old wish books," known today as catalogues, were a cowhand's library. Literature was mighty scarce out West, so cowhands read and reread the old wish books filled with pictures of boots, saddles, hats, and such. If a cowgirl couldn't get her hands on a wish book, then she might just memorize the printing on canned goods. Cowhands would quiz each other about the ingredients listed on the cans as a sort of reading and memory game.

P is for plains.

Plains, plateaus, and prairies make up good grazing land for a cowgirl's cattle. Before fences, cowhands drove their cattle 'round the wide-open spaces, searching out the richest grass. Now cattle are held in pastures irrigated by nearby streams.

Q is for quarter horse.

A cowgirl's closest friend is her **q**uarter horse. **Q**uarter horses are **q**uick, smart, hardworking, muscular horses that can outrun any other breed in a **q**uarter-mile race. A **q**uarter horse's endurance under the saddle is a trait his cowgirl appreciates as much as a **q**uail in the pot at the end of the day.

R is for rodeo.

A **r**odeo gives a gal a chance to show her skill at **r**oping and **r**iding. While barrel **r**acing, a cowgirl needs to stick to her horse like hair on a cow. **R**odeo gals competing in **r**elay **r**aces and team **r**oping events get a cowgirl's heart beating and bring crowds to their feet.

S is for saddle.

A cowgirl's saddle is as important as air. A good Western saddle is necessary for a cowgirl to work, and at the end of the day, it can be used for a pillow when she sleeps under the starry Texas sky.

T is for trick riders.

Trick riders dazzle the circuit crowds across these here United States. Most cowgirls began riding before they took to walking. There wasn't anything they couldn't do, as long as it could be done on the back of a horse.

U is for underhand pitch.

The **u**nderhand pitch of a cowgirl's rope heels a calf without setting the others into a stampede. She'll throw under the calf's belly so that li'l calf will two-step right **u**p into the loop. Then that gal will give a tug and drop that calf right on the spot. Then she will vaccinate and brand it all in one swift ballet of action.

V is for vaqueros.

Before cowboys and cowgirls there were Mexican vaqueros. The Spanish brought horses and cattle to these here Americas. The vaqueros handled the herds of cattle on horseback. These Spanish-speaking Mexicans followed the cattle right out of Mexico and into Texas and California. American Revolutionary veterans, adventurers, and settlers learned cattlemen skills from vaqueros and went on to become our own venturesome cowhands.

W is for Wild West show.

Wild West shows made cowgirls such as sharpshooting Annie Oakley and trick-riding Tad Lukas famous. The Wild West shows allowed free-spirited cowgirls to prove they were as tough as a bull's hide and as talented as Hollywood movie stars.

X is for XIT brand.

Cowgirls are taught to read a brand before they learn to read a book. Brands take the alphabet one step beyond elementary schoolin' by adding wings, feet, rockers, bars, circles, or numbers or by slanting the letter or laying it on its side. People know a man's brand before they remember his name. **XIT** ("Ten in Texas") is just one famous brand.

Y is for yarn.

Cowgirls and cowboys too love to spin a **yarn** while sitting 'round a campfire. These stories are known to embroider reality and stitch characters bigger than Texas. The first **yarn**-teller starts off a tale, and the next one stretches the hide of that story to top the first. All that storytelling leads to a lot of **yee**-haws and **yippee-yi-yo**s!

Z is for cowgirl Zelda from Zanesville brushing her zebra dun.

Y'all can zigzag across these United States and find cowgirls in every state: Carla in California showing her calf for 4-H, Kelsey in Kansas kicking it up in the dancehall, Sam in South Dakota demonstrating her shooting skills, Winnie in Washington riding in a Wild West show. What they have in common is that they are all American gals, just like you, with a cowgirl's zest for life.